Symbols of Freedom

National Parks

Yellowstone National Park

M.C. Hall

Heinemann Library
Chicago, Illinois

Customer Service 888-454-2279
Visit our website at www.heinemannlibrary.com

Page layout by Richard Parker and Maverick Design
Photo research by Maria Joannou
Illustrations by Jeff Edwards
Printed and bound in China by South China Printing Company Limited

10 09 08 07 06
10 9 8 7 6 5 4 3 2 1

Library of Congress Cataloging-in-Publication Data
Hall, Margaret, 1947-
   Yellowstone National Park / Margaret Hall.
      p. cm. -- (National parks)
Includes bibliographical references and index.
ISBN 1-4034-6702-1 (library binding-hardcover) -- ISBN 1-4034-6709-9 (pbk.)
1. Yellowstone National Park--Juvenile literature. I. Title. II. Series.
   F722.H255 2005
   978.7'52033--dc22
                      2004030391

Acknowledgments
The author and publishers are grateful to the following for permission to reproduce copyright material:
Alamy pp. 4 (Andre Jenny), 16 (David Copeman); Corbis pp. 22, 29, 30, 31, 32, 24 (Kennan Ward), 19 (Kevin R. Morris), 13 (Lester Lefkowitz), 20 (Raymond Gehman), 17 (W. Perry Conway); Creatas p. 7; Creatas/Brand X p. 18; Denver Public Library p. 8 (Western History & Geneology Photo Collection/ Colorado Historical Society); Getty Images/The Image Bank p. 10; National Park Service pp. 5, 9, 11, 12, 14, 15, 21, 23, 25, 26, 27

Cover photograph of Yellowstone Falls reproduced with permission of Creatas

Every effort has been made to contact copyright holders of any material reproduced in this book.
Any omissions will be rectified in subsequent printings if notice is given to the publisher.

Some words are shown in bold, **like this**. You can find out what they mean by looking in the glossary.

Contents

Our National Parks

National parks are areas of land that are set aside for people to visit and enjoy **nature**. National parks do not belong to one person. They belong to all the people of the United States.

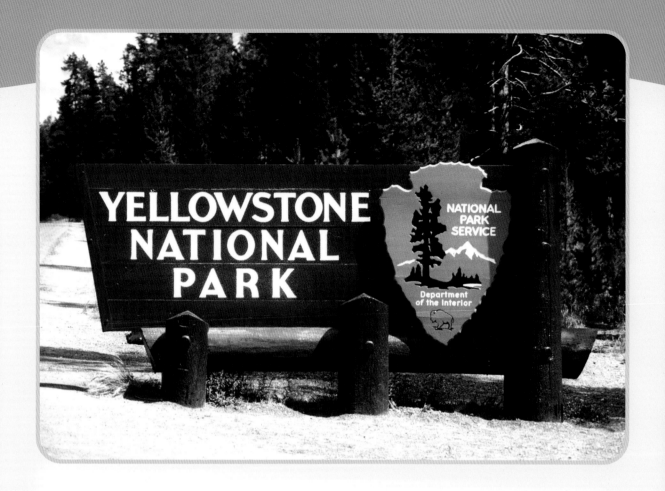

There are more than 50 national parks in the United States. Yellowstone National Park was the first national park. Every year millions of people from around the world visit Yellowstone.

Yellowstone National Park

Yellowstone National Park is in the western part of the United States. Most of Yellowstone is located in Wyoming. Small parts of the park are also located in Montana and Idaho.

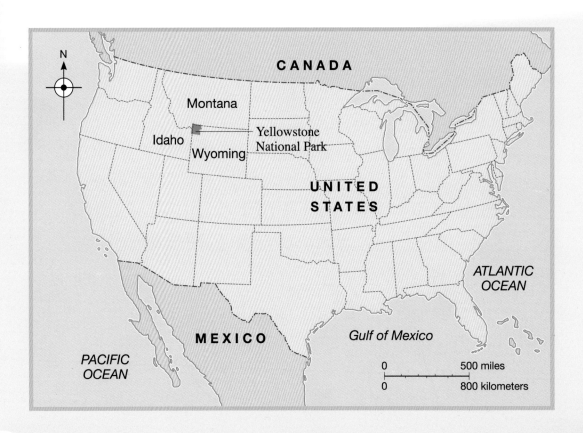

Yellowstone is one of the largest **national parks** in the United States. It is larger than the states of Delaware and Rhode Island together! Yellowstone gets its name from the yellow rock that is found in the area.

Native Americans were the first people to live in Yellowstone. Later, **fur trappers** came to the area. They told stories about steaming pools of water. Soon other people came to see if the stories were true.

Early visitors to Yellowstone came by stagecoach.

The United States **government** sent explorers to Yellowstone. They brought back pictures and paintings of the area. In 1872 the government made Yellowstone a **national park**.

Visiting Yellowstone National Park

Most people visit Yellowstone National Park in July and August, when the weather is warm. Visitors camp, hike, fish, and watch **wildlife**. They also view **geysers**, **hot springs**, and other unusual sights.

Yellowstone is very cold in the winter. Most park roads close because of the snow. Some people still visit Yellowstone in the winter. They come to **snowshoe**, cross-country ski, and ride snowmobiles.

Geysers

Yellowstone has many **geysers**. A geyser is a fountain of hot water and steam. The water and steam build up underground. Then they **erupt** out of cracks in the earth's crust.

There are more than 300 geysers in Yellowstone.

Old Faithful is Yellowstone's most famous geyser. Most geysers only erupt once in a while, so visitors often miss these geysers. Old Faithful erupts about once an hour.

Water from Old Faithful shoots high into the air.

Hot Springs and Mud Pots

Minerals in the water make interesting shapes around the rocks.

Yellowstone has thousands of **hot springs**. The springs form when hot water bubbles up out of cracks in the earth. The water makes steaming pools or flows over rocks.

When water from a hot spring mixes with dirt, it makes hot mud. Pools of hot mud at Yellowstone National Park are called mud pots. Sometimes mud pots bubble like oatmeal cooking on the stove!

Mountains and Rivers

The Rocky Mountains ring Yellowstone National Park. A few mountain peaks are tall enough to be covered in snow all year.

There are many rivers in Yellowstone Park. The most famous river is the Yellowstone River. In the mountains, the Yellowstone River flows through a deep **canyon**. Many people visit the Grand Canyon of the Yellowstone.

Waterfalls and Lakes

The Lower Falls

Two of the most beautiful sights in Yellowstone National Park are waterfalls. The Upper Falls and The Lower Falls are close together on the Yellowstone River.

The Yellowstone River flows into a large valley in the middle of the park. Here, the river forms a huge lake. Visitors come to Yellowstone Lake to fish, swim, and go boating.

Yellowstone's Plants

Most of Yellowstone National Park is covered by forests of aspen and pine trees. There are also many large **meadows** filled with grass and wildflowers.

This meadow is full of lupines and other wildflowers.

In 1988 lightning started a huge forest fire in Yellowstone. The fire destroyed large parts of the forest. Soon after the fire, plants started to grow back.

Yellowstone's Animals

Many animals roam freely in Yellowstone. Bison, elk, moose, and deer live in the forests and **meadows**. Bighorn sheep, bobcats, and mountain lions live in the mountains.

This herd of bison is crossing Yellowstone River.

Many bears also live in Yellowstone's forests and meadows. Visitors sometimes see black bears near the park roads. Grizzly bears usually stay away from people.

A young black bear sits by the side of a road in Yellowstone.

Bringing Back the Wolves

Early park visitors were afraid of the wolves in Yellowstone. The animals were trapped and taken away. Some were killed. Before long, there were no wolves in Yellowstone.

This wolf is being released back into the wild.

Today, people understand that wolves belong in the park. In 1995 a few gray wolves were brought back to Yellowstone. Now there are almost 200 wolves living in the park.

Park Buildings and People

There are five visitor centers in Yellowstone. People visit to get information or to buy supplies. There is also a large hotel called the Old Faithful Inn. The inn is more than 100 years old!

Yellowstone has many **park rangers**. These men and women lead **nature** tours and hikes. The rangers teach visitors about the plants, animals, and other wonderful sights of the park.

Map of Yellowstone National Park

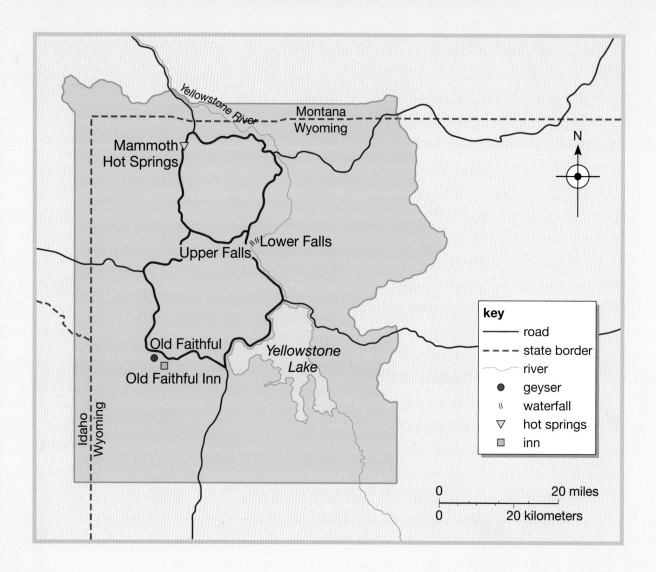

Yellowstone River

Montana
Wyoming

Mammoth
Hot Springs

N

Upper Falls
Lower Falls

Old Faithful

Old Faithful Inn

Yellowstone
Lake

Idaho
Wyoming

key

—— road
- - - state border
～～ river
● geyser
\\\ waterfall
▽ hot springs
■ inn

0   20 miles
0   20 kilometers

Timeline

640,000 years ago	Volcanic eruption creates land that will be Yellowstone
12,000 years ago	Native Americans begin to live in Yellowstone area
About 1807	First white man comes to Yellowstone
1871	United States **government** sends groups to explore Yellowstone
1872	Yellowstone becomes a **national park**
1877–1882	The first roads are built in Yellowstone
1883	Railroad lines are built up to the park entrance
1916	United States government creates the National Park Service to care for the parks
1918	The first **park rangers** begin working at Yellowstone
1959	Large earthquake destroys parts of Yellowstone
1988	Fire destroys large areas of forest
1995	Wolves are brought back to Yellowstone National Park

Glossary

canyon very steep valley

erupt to shoot up into the air

fur trapper person who traps animals and sells the fur

geyser fountain of hot water and steam

government group of people that makes laws for and runs a country

hot spring hot water that bubbles up from inside the earth

meadow grassy field with few or no trees

mineral natural material found in rocks, soil, and water. Minerals can build up on surfaces that water touches.

national park natural area set aside by the government for people to visit

nature the outdoors and the wild plants and animals found there

park ranger man or woman who works in a national park and shares information about the wildlife and unusual sights of the park

snowshoe to travel on top of the snow on snowshoes that are attached to boots

wildlife wild animals of an area

Find Out More

Books

An older reader can help you with these books:

Compton, Carrie L. *A to Z Yellowstone National Park*. Portland, Ore.: WW West, 2004.

Graf, Mike. *Yellowstone National Park*. Mankato, Minn.: Capstone, 2003.

Halvorsen, Lisa. *Yellowstone: Letters Home from Our National Parks*. San Diego, Calif.: Blackbirch Press, 2000.

Klingel, Cynthia. *Yellowstone National Park*. Chanhassen, Minn.: Child's World, 2000.

Meister, Cari. *Yellowstone National Park*. Mankato, Minn.: Checkerboard Books, 2000.

Pecorella, Jane. *Yellowstone: Our First National Park*. New York, N.Y.: Rosen, 2002.

Address

To find out more about Yellowstone National Park, write to:

Yellowstone National Park
P.O. Box 168
Yellowstone National Park, WY 82190-0168

Index